To

_____

From

_____

Copyright © 2008 Simple Truths, LLC

Copyright © 2008 BJ Gallagher

Published by SimpleTruths, LLC
1952 McDowell Road
Naperville, Illinois 60563

Design: Lynn Harker, Simple Truths, Illinois
Illusrations by Sam Weiss

Simple Truths is a registered trademark.
Printed and bound in the United States of America

ISBN: 978-1-60810-007-1

800-900-3427
www.simpletruths.com

02 WOZ 08

A peacock IN THE LAND OF **PENGUINS**

A Story about Courage in Creating a Land
of Opportunity

**BJ Gallagher
and Warren H. Schmidt**

Foreword by Ken Blanchard

We dedicate this book
to all who yearn to fly free
and show their true colors –
and to all who have the wisdom
to learn from those who are different.

FOREWORD

Every once in a while a small book comes along that deals with a profound subject in a simple, elegant way. *A Peacock in the Land of Penguins* is such a book. I loved this book when the first edition came out in 1995, and I love this new edition even more. It provides important insights into the issue of creativity and innovation in the workplace – and it does so in a most engaging manner. Through the medium of a fable, this book helps us to see what can happen when we try to express ourselves fully and courageously in an environment created by executives and managers who view the world very differently.

Stories are a great way to convey important messages – they inspire and teach at the same time. People forget facts, figures and theories, but they remember stories. People who know me can tell you how often I use stories in my own conversations, in my speeches, and in my daily life. I love to write great stories, and I love to read great stories.

This is the story of Perry the Peacock – a bright, talented, colorful bird – who comes to live in the Land of Penguins. He soon runs into problems because the penguins have established a chilly organizational climate that is formal, bureaucratic, and governed by a vast array of written and unwritten rules. Although his talent is recognized, his different and unusual style makes the penguins feel uneasy. The very thing that he was recruited for – his distinctive flair and creativity – is now viewed as a "problem" by the penguins, once Perry is inside the organization!

His experience reflects that of "birds of a different feather" in many of today's organizations. While executives and managers today say that they want new ideas and new thinking from their employees, their actions indicate otherwise. New ideas are disruptive, they're messy, they challenge the status quo, they require taking chances and increased risk, and they push everyone out of their comfort zones. So people who are different, people with new views on how to make the organization successful, are often discouraged from expressing them – much to the detriment of both the individual and the organization.

This delightful corporate fable follows the adventures of Perry the Peacock and other exotic birds as they try to make their way in the Land of Penguins. Their story is both entertaining and enlightening. This is a tale of the perils and possibilities of being unique and creative in a world that values comfort, safety, and the predictability of conformity.

If you're interested in new ideas for making yourself and your organizations successful, read this little book. Creating a workplace where new ideas and innovation can flourish is a top priority for managers and employees alike. There are important insights for all of us!

Ken Blanchard
Co-author of *The One Minute Manager*

There once was a time,
in the not so distant past,
when penguins ruled many lands
in the Sea of Organizations.

These penguins were not always wise,
they were not always popular,
but they were always in charge.

Most organizations looked the same:

Top executives
and managers
	wore their distinctive penguin suits,
while worker birds
of many kinds
	wore colors and outfits
	that reflected their work
	and their lifestyles.

Birds who aspired to move up
in their organizations
were encouraged to become
as penguin-like as possible –
	to shorten their steps
		and learn the penguin stride,
			to wear penguin suits,
		and follow
			the example of their leaders.

Employee Development Departments
offered
extensive training programs
on appropriate penguin-like behavior.

The rules
and norms
were clear
from Day One.

Penguins advised in subtle
(and not so subtle) ways:

"This is the way we do things here."

"If you want to be successful,
  be like us."

Some birds
who wanted to move up
in the pecking order
became very good
at taking on the penguin look
and penguin behaviors.

But even *they*
found that
they never quite
made it
into key positions.

It was assumed by all
that penguins
were natural leaders –
    orderly, loyal,
        and good team players.

Penguins could be trusted
to put
the organization's interests
ahead
of personal and family concerns.

Other birds
were thought to be
more flighty
and less dependable.

Of course,
this was never stated
out loud
or in writing.

Because,
    like every organization,
penguins wanted to be seen
as fair-minded and
ready to promote
on the basis of
    talent,
    hard work,
    and contribution.

But everyone really knew —
the penguins
had always been in charge,
    and
the penguins
***would** always be in charge.*

The elder penguins
would take
younger penguins
under their wings
and coach them
on
how to be successful.

They would invite them
    to play golf
        and go jogging.
They would sit together
in the executive dining room
    and talk about sports.

It was clear to everyone
who the important penguins were.

It was also clear
that the penguins
felt most comfortable
around each other.

Life was harmonious
in the Land of Penguins,
     as long as everyone played
     by the penguins' rules.

Other birds
in the organization
knew how to act
to make the penguins
feel comfortable
and secure.

But there came a time
when things began to change
in the Land of Penguins ...

Senior penguins
started to visit
other lands
where they encountered
interesting birds
who impressed them
with their
management talent,
    experience,
        and accomplishments.

"These birds are not penguins,"
   the elders thought,

"but perhaps
  they could become penguins
  if we brought them to our land
  and trained them
  in our penguin ways."

"Surely
  these impressive and unusual birds
  could adapt to life
  in the Land of Penguins,
  and the talent
  they bring
  would make us
  even more successful."

"Our climate is different –
  chilly and cold.
  And our terrain is unique –
  icy and barren."

"But we have thrived there
  and so perhaps
  will these new birds."

"If they are as smart
  as we think they are,
  they can adjust
  to our weather and our ways."

And this was how
Perry the Peacock
came to live
in the Land of Penguins ...

Now
Perry was clearly
    not a penguin.

In fact,
    he was the antithesis of penguinity –

Perry was a peacock –
    a bright, colorful and noisy bird.

Perry was a very talented peacock,
who had accomplished
some very impressive things
in his own land.

He could write well
and was excellent at managing his budgets.
He was creative and imaginative,
and at the same time,
practical and sensible.

He had many friends and admirers
in his own land,
and was very popular and well-liked.

Senior managers
in the Land of Penguins
were intrigued
    when they met Perry the Peacock.

They knew that he was different –
but they were impressed
with what he had achieved in his career,
and they were fascinated
with the possibilities
that he represented.

They felt that Perry
    had real Penguin Potential.

Perry,
    in turn,
was attracted to the penguins
because of the great things
he had heard and read
about their land –
    the promise of status,
      and wealth,
    and a sense of belonging
      to a great and powerful enterprise.

It was a rich land –
    and all the birds
      were paid extremely well.

"My future will be brighter,"
    he thought,
"in this new land."

And so the penguins
and the peacock
agreed.

He would join them,
and together
they would achieve
great things.

At first
   everyone was delighted.

The penguins were pleased
and impressed
   with their new recruit.

He stood out
from the crowd
in the way he sparkled
and displayed flashes of color
every now and then.

And Perry was pleased, too,
with the novelty
and the newness.

He was impressed
by the penguins –
they looked so important
in their black and white suits,
especially
when they gathered together
for meetings
and company events.

Their formality and manners
were so different
from anything
he had ever seen
or experienced
before.

Now the peacock
was careful
in the beginning
  not to display
    too much of his colorful nature.

You see,
some friends
in his own land
had warned Perry
about penguins —

They had cautioned him
about the rules
and the style
with which the penguins
governed their land.

So he kept his feathers
folded up
much of the time,
and would only occasionally
flash them open
to dazzle the penguins
with the full range
of his talent and color.

He wanted
to be taken seriously
and he wanted
to be successful.

So he subdued
his own peacock nature
for a while,
until he could be sure
that the penguins
had accepted him
completely.

He was confident
that when he produced
good results for them,
they would embrace him fully –
    in all his peacock glory –
and he could relax
    and just be himself.

You see,
things were very different
in the land where he had grown up –
the Land of Learning.

In the Land of Learning
there were LOTS of different kinds of birds.

There were wise birds (owls),
and powerful birds (eagles),
and hunting birds (hawks),
improbable birds (ostriches),
elegant birds (swans),
and awkward birds (gooney birds).

It was crowded and noisy,
    with a buzz of activity
    and the rough and tumble
        of competition.

Birds had to work hard,
    learn fast,
        and live by their wits
        and creativity
            in order to be successful.

It was an exhilarating
    but tough environment!

The motto in the Land of Learning was:

Imagine it.
Try it.
Prove it.
<u>Do</u> it!

All the birds
worked hard
to prove their talent
and earn their place
    in the sun.

In the Land of Learning
the birds didn't always
get along peaceably.

Sometimes there were
conflicts and differences,
struggles and irritations.

But conflicts and differences
were valued
    because the birds believed
    that that's how new ideas get tested.

Discussion
    and debate
        and argument
was the way
    change was introduced
and progress was made.

Nobody cared
if you were a penguin or a peacock,
    a dove or a blue jay.

Being smart
    and talented
        and productive
was all that mattered.

Initiative,
    creativity,
        and results
were most highly prized.

It was what was inside you
and what you contributed
that counted –
    not the kind or color
    of feathers you wore.

But Perry the Peacock
was in for
some very different challenges
when he left
the Land of Learning
and went to work
in the Land of Penguins.

He was used to hard work
    and fighting for his ideas
        and competing
with many different kinds of birds.

But nothing in his background
had prepared him for
the unique ways
and special customs
of the Land of Penguins.

He wanted to do well
    and be successful.

He was flattered
that these powerful and prestigious penguins
had recruited him
into their ranks,
    and he wanted to please them.

He studied the penguins' walk,
   their talk
      and their style.

"How strange,"
   he thought to himself,
"they all look alike.
   They're like clones of each other."

He was intrigued
   and puzzled
      at the same time.

And as time went on, his troubles began ...

Some of the penguins
began to grumble
that his distinctive peacock voice
was too loud.

You see,
penguins speak
in very subdued,
modulated
tones,
and the peacock's laughter
and excited exclamations
startled their time-honored
sense of propriety.

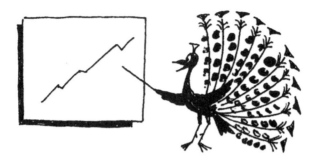

His feathers began to show
more and more all the time,
    as he worked hard
    and accomplished
    many great things.

Everyone agreed
that he was quite talented
and productive,
    and they liked the impressive results
    of his work.

But his flashy, colorful style
made some
of the senior penguins
uneasy.

Many of the other penguins
in the land
were delighted
with this new and unusual bird
in their midst.

They called him
"a breath of fresh air"
　　　and welcomed his exuberance.

Some of the junior penguins
privately speculated
about how long he would last
in the Land of Penguins.
They saw
how un-penguin-like he was,
and wondered how long
this would be tolerated by the elders.

A couple of the senior penguins
tried to take him under their wings
and coach him.

"Look," they said,
"we like your work,
  but some of the elders
  are uncomfortable with your style."

"You need to change to be accepted here."

"Why don't you put on a penguin suit,
  so you look more like us?"

"It doesn't fit,"
   responded Perry the Peacock.

"It's too tight and constraining.
 My tail feathers will get crushed
 and my wings can't move well."

"I can't work if I'm not comfortable."

The elders said,
"Well then,
  maybe you could paint your feathers
  black and white,
  like ours."

"Then at least
  you wouldn't look
  quite so different."

"What's wrong with the way I am?"
    Perry asked.

He was hurt and confused.

"I work hard,
  I produce great results –
  everyone says so."

"Why can't you look at my work
  rather than my feathers?"

"Aren't my accomplishments
  more important
        than my style?"

"It's such a small thing,"
    the penguins responded.

"You are smart and talented.
  You could have a bright future here.
  You just need to act
  more like us
  and then
  the elders will be more comfortable."

"You need to wear a penguin suit,
  and soften your voice,
    and shorten your steps."

"Just watch all the other penguins –
  see how they act?"

"Try to be like the rest of us."

Perry believed
that their intentions were good,
    but their words wounded him nonetheless.

"Why can't I just be who I am?
 Why do I have to change
 to be accepted by you?"
    he asked.

"That's just the way things are here,"
the penguins shrugged.

"It's the same everywhere
in the Sea of Organizations."

He suspected they might be right,
but his heart didn't want to accept it.

He thanked them
for their words of advice
and their concern for him,
and he went back to his nest
to think things over.

As the months rolled by,
he discussed his dilemma
with some of the other birds he trusted.

Several of them
were also new birds
who had been recruited
around the same time as
Perry's arrival
in the Land of Penguins.

Many of them
were experiencing
similar kinds
of problems ...

Edward the Eagle
complained that he, too,
was getting pressure
to change.

He was smart and powerful
and very skilled at his work,
and he even wore the requisite penguin suit.

But Edward didn't talk
or act like a penguin,
and this bothered the elders.

They were embarrassed
by his accent,
and sent him to
a prestigious,
tradition-steeped
Eastern Business School
for special executive penguin training.

But it didn't work –
   he was still an eagle in penguin's clothing.

He couldn't change who he was.

And Helen the Hawk
had similar problems.

She was beautiful and powerful –
    smart, sharp and aggressive.
She was a skilled hunter,
    with fierce competitive instincts.

She wore her penguin suit,
occasionally more colorful
than the male penguins,
but still acceptable.

Helen tried to adapt
to the style of the penguins,
     but her hawk-like nature
     would always reveal itself.

Her talons were sharp,
     her eyes piercing,
          her manner intense,
               her hunter's instincts
               ever alert.

And her aggressive style
     made the elders very uncomfortable.

It was the same story
   with Mike the Mockingbird.

He was an especially brilliant bird –
   creative,
      imaginative,
         and impulsive.
He was attracted by sparkling ideas.

He flew fast,
   worked hard,
      and jumped around
making good things happen
   all over the Land of Penguins.

But Mike soon discovered that
penguins are territorial birds,
who build their empires,
    establish their pecking order,
        and fiercely resent anyone
        who comes into their turf
        without being properly invited.

Since Mike was not a penguin,
he was not sensitive
to the politics
and the turf issues
of the senior penguins.

With his penchant for creativity
and imagining possibilities
outside the ordinary,
    he sometimes offended
    some of the elders
    by flying into their territories.

They were threatened and annoyed
    at his intrusions.

Like Edward the Eagle
and Helen the Hawk,
Mike wore his penguin suit
and tried his best
to learn the ways of the penguins
so he would be accepted by them.

But ultimately,
     he could not change who he really was.

The story was similar
   with Sara the Swan.

She was an optimistic dreamer,
with unusual visions
for the future
of the Land of Penguins.

She had interesting ideas,
   unique ideas,
     good ideas –

but her ideas
often were not heard
because she expressed them
   in such a gentle way.

Her style was graceful,
   her manner gracious,
     but the penguins
     had doubts about
       her toughness
       and her strength.

There were others as well...

The thing they all had in common
was that none of them
had grown up
in the Land of Penguins.

They had been
recruited and hired
from other places.

The penguin elders
had enticed these outsiders
with promises of success:

"We want your fresh thinking
   and new ideas.
   We admire your track record
   and want you to do
   great things for us."

But,
as soon as the new birds
were inside the organization,
the elders issued them
penguin suits
and began pressuring them
to talk,
      act,
            and think
more like penguins.

The penguins said,
"We value diversity."

But their actions said otherwise.

As the exotic new birds
discussed
their mutual frustrations
among themselves,
they tried
to figure out
what to do.

Several of them
decided to try
to change the culture
   rather than
   let the culture change them.

"We'll work on our bosses, and other
 key penguins,"
   they vowed,
"without
 being too obvious,
 of course."

They each
developed strategies
for becoming
Agents of Change
   within the Land of Penguins.

Edward the Eagle
adopted a ***"Strategy of Support:"***

> ***"Catch your boss***
> ***doing something right ...***
> ***(or approximately right!)"***

Whenever his boss
accepted
any new idea,
Edward would reinforce him
by saying,
"I appreciate
your willingness
to try
something different.
Your support
makes my job
interesting
and rewarding."

Helen the Hawk
had her own ideas
about how to bring about change.
She used a "Strategy of Hopeful Thinking:"

> *"Act on the basis*
> *of assumptions*
> *you'd **like** to be true.*
> *(with caution, of course!)"*

Helen would regularly send
her boss newspaper clippings and magazine articles
with a personal note
which read:
"Because of your continuing interest
in learning new ways to handle our marketing,
I thought
you'd like to see the attached article
about Prosperous Enterprise, Inc.
in the recent issue of
the 'Journal of Successful Organizations.'"

Mike the Mockingbird
decided he would try
an extremely bold strategy –
a *"Strategy of Calculated Ignorance:"*

> *"Violate*
> *penguin policy –*
> *and if caught –*
> *use the Puzzled Prodigal Response."*

Whenever Mike was questioned
about making a particular decision,
he would assume
an expression of puzzlement
as he described
how a shortcut
would achieve something
that everyone
had agreed
was important.

Sara the Swan,
being much gentler
in her approach,
tried a **_"Strategy of Safe Learning:"_**

> **_"Expose
> the Senior Penguins
> to new ideas
> in settings
> where
> they won't be embarrassed
> by having to respond."_**

Sara would casually mention
her ideas and suggestions
in quiet conversations
and informal settings.

She planted ideas,
nurtured them slowly,
and watched for progress.

Some of the other birds –
   who were determined
     to transform themselves –
tried very hard
to become penguins.

They walked the penguin walk;
   they talked the penguin talk.

They preened
   and practiced
     to produce the desired result.

But ultimately they failed,
because
   they couldn't change
   who they really were.

And a few birds,
like Perry,
didn't even try
to become a penguin.

Perry just knew
in his heart
that there must be
at least *one* land in
the vast Sea of Organizations
where
he could be a peacock
and be valued
for his uniqueness.

He resisted
the penguins' advice and pressure,
firm in his conviction
that he should be valued
for his results.

Over time,
things got worse
for Perry
and the other exotic birds
in the Land of Penguins ...

Their strategies
to change
the penguin way of doing things
met with
resistance and red tape.

Their ideas and efforts
were discounted
and dismissed.

Their questions of "Why?"
were answered with:
  "This is the way
    we've *always* done things here."

The exotic birds learned
through painful experience
that the culture
of the land
was deeply entrenched.

The structures and systems
were rigid and unbending.
Policies and procedures
ensured the continuity
of the penguin practices.

It eventually became clear
that individual efforts
at persuasion and influence
were foolish and futile
in the face of such
longstanding tradition
and structure.

The exotic birds realized
that the penguin ways
had developed
over many years
and would not change
easily or soon.

Their strategies
to change themselves
also fell short,
because
deep down inside
they just weren't penguins.

**They couldn't change
who they really were.**

Their hearts were filled
with frustration,
    disappointment,
        and sadness.

They had come
to the Land of Penguins
with such high hopes
and great expectations.

They had wanted to contribute
    and be successful.

But what they got instead was quiet criticism,
     stifling conformity,
          and subtle rejection.

And so,
one by one,
Perry and the other new birds
each began to realize
the same thing –

They could not be themselves
in the Land of Penguins.

They had to move on.

They knew their futures
lay somewhere else
in the vast Sea of Organizations.

Some of the new birds
left the Land of Penguins
on their own.

Others
were pushed out
by the senior penguins,
who said,
"You make us too uncomfortable.
  You don't fit here.
  You must leave."

Whether they left on their own
or were forced out by the elders,
all the departing birds
shared one thing in common –
   the pain and confusion
   of being different,
     and the sadness
     and disappointment
     of not being accepted
     for who they were.

These birds of a different feather
had all struggled
with the same dilemma:

How much
could they
or would they
change to "fit in"
and be accepted
in the Land of Penguins,
and how much
could they be themselves?

What price would they pay to be successful?

And the penguins had their own dilemma:

*How much diversity
could they tolerate in their land
and still maintain
their own comfort level?*

*Wouldn't all these differences
endanger
their harmonious corporate culture?*

The penguins,
after all,
had enjoyed
many years of profitable success
by following
historic penguin traditions
and ways of doing business.

They were reluctant
to change the style
that had made them great.

And they were disappointed
that so many
of their new recruits
did not work out.

Perry the Peacock
was the first to leave.

He had many friends
from other lands,
and they told him
of a new and wondrous place
they had visited in their travels.

They described it as
"the Land of Opportunity."

There,
they told him,
his work
and his contributions
would be valued –
   and his uniqueness
   would be applauded,
      not criticized.

He could be
   colorful,
      flamboyant,
         and enthusiastic,
and others would appreciate him
   for his distinctive style.

Dare he hope
that these reports were true?

Was this the place
he had longed for?

He had to go
and see for himself.

When Perry arrived in
the Land of Opportunity
he found that it
was totally different
from the Land of Penguins…

Here,
workers and bosses
didn't waste
time and energy
pretending to be
something different
from what they were.

They knew
that they needed
many kinds of different birds
in order to thrive
in the turbulent and competitive
Sea of Organizations.

And they knew that
the most important requirement
for organizational success
is acceptance and trust.

It is acceptance and trust
that make it possible
for each bird
to sing its own song –
    confident that it will be heard –
        even by those
        who sing with a different voice.

All the birds
expressed themselves freely,
and their lively exchanges
of differing views
ensured
that their work
and their ways
were constantly improving.

Best of all,
they had confidence
in their leaders,
birds of many kinds
who had risen to their positions
through talent,
    skill,
        and ability.

The motto here was:

Some birds swam,
  many flew,
    and some kept their feet
    planted firmly on the ground.

This gave them
many different perspectives
on the world –
  which they shared
  easily and openly
  with one another.

Their shared knowledge made them wise.
And their wisdom made them successful.

Perry knew
he had found his new home.

As the months and years
rolled by,
one by one,
Edward the Eagle,
Helen the Hawk,
Mike the Mockingbird,
and Sara the Swan
also made their way
to the Land of Opportunity.

They had heard from Perry
about the freedom
and openness
that existed there.

In this land,
Edward could fly free and high,
    soaring as fast
        as his wings could carry him.

Others admired
his grace and power –
and commented
on what an inspiration he was
to younger birds
who came from humble beginnings
but had ambitious dreams
of flying high someday themselves.

Nobody even noticed
the way he spoke,
    with his unique accent.

Helen,
who had rattled the penguins
with her intensity
and her keen competitive instincts,
found a place
where she was welcome
in the Land of Opportunity.

Her colleagues
valued her hunting skills
and her ability to spot
changing trends
and possibilities
for new ventures.

They commented frequently
    on her elegant beauty
        and distinctive style.

She was perfectly suited
for her new position
in the Land of Opportunity.

Mike
at long last
experienced the creative joy
of jumping from project to project,
   working hard and fast,
      and stirring up new ideas
      wherever he went.

No longer fettered
by a rigid pecking order
and boundaries
dictated by penguins,
his productivity skyrocketed –
   and others marveled
      at his amazing skills.

Sara, too,
found the Land of Opportunity
to be a hospitable place
for her dreamy,
   reflective,
      imaginative
style of working.

She started writing
and pursuing ideas
in ways
she once thought
would never be possible
in a place of work.

Other birds flocked to her,
wanting to work with her
and share in the realization
of her dreams.

She was appreciated
for the freedom
she allowed others,
and
for her gentle style.

These diverse birds
all prospered and grew
as never before.

They felt affirmed and appreciated
by the admiration
of the other birds
in the land.

They experienced a new freedom,
    allowing them to fly,
        each with their own unique style.

They worked hard –
    and enjoyed
    the fruits of their labors.

Above all else,
they knew the joy of just being themselves.

Perry the Peacock flashed his colorful feathers;

Edward the Eagle soared with power and grace;

Helen the Hawk skillfully kept watch and hunted;

Mike the Mockingbird followed his creative
instincts and innovative ideas;

And Sara the Swan drifted and floated
with the currents.

Perry and his friends
found that
life was good and
their future was bright
in the Land of Opportunity.

There
they could all succeed –
    each with a unique and different style –
and make contributions
that would be welcomed and appreciated
by their colleagues
and co-workers.

They came to realize
that the Land of Opportunity
is more than a place...

It is a state of mind.

The Land of Opportunity is an attitude.

It is
an openness to new ideas,
    a willingness to listen,
        an eagerness to learn,
            a desire to grow,
and the flexibility to change.

The Land of Opportunity
is a new way of dealing with each other.

It becomes a reality
when we stop judging each other
by superficial criteria
and begin to see
and appreciate
everyone
as uniquely
talented,
capable,
and valuable.

The Land of Opportunity
is where we live and work
when we choose
to see with new eyes,
     live from our hearts,
     and allow ourselves
     and others
     to be what we truly are ...

Ourselves.

The End

AFTERWORD

…and what of the Land of Penguins?

Their story continues to unfold every day
in corporations and organizations
across the country …

AUTHOR
BJ GALLAGHER

BJ Gallagher is in many ways like the lead character in this fable – colorful and extravagant, noisy and messy – a bird who is difficult to ignore. She is a free spirit who loves her work – a child of the 60's, who sees her mission in life as "comforting the afflicted, and afflicting the comfortable" (a line she once heard in a good sermon). She does both of them very well – especially the latter. She is a human potential missionary who hangs out in corporations and other organizations, showing people how they can do well by doing good.

Her USC doctoral studies in Social Ethics equipped her to be a professional do-gooder, while her years in the business world taught her to speak the language of the bottom line. She considers herself to be a pragmatic idealist. Her undergraduate training in the social sciences taught her to observe, listen, ask good questions, and analyze human behavior in all its complexity and paradoxes – great preparation for a life in business!

BJ was reluctant to leave the academic nest (she wanted to be a professor when she grew up), and spent seven years on the staff at USC – her last position there was Director of Staff Training and Professional Development. While she was supposed to be writing her dissertation, she wrote a book called *Telling Your Story, Exploring Your Faith* (it paid better and was more fun, too).

She finally decided to try her wings in the "real world" of business, and landed at *The Los Angeles Times,* where she spent almost five years as the Manager of Training and Development. It was at the newspaper that she developed a keen interest in studying other types of "birds," and she learned a lot while directing training programs and consulting projects for the company. She left *The Times* in 1991 to form her own consulting and training company, Peacock Productions.

Like any good peacock, BJ loves an audience, and is a popular workshop leader and public speaker. She really shows her true colors when she's talking about some of her favorite subjects: personal accountability, dealing with change, tapping into the creativity of diversity, male/female communications, success strategies for women, and her all-time favorite – how to manage your boss. She also consults with organizations on other human resource issues – teambuilding, employee surveys, creating a culture of pluralism, among others. She has managed to put on her penguin suit often enough to work with many respectable corporate and nonprofit clients, including IBM, Chrysler, Chevron, Southern California Edison, the American Press Institute, the City of Santa Monica, and the American Lung Association.

This iridescent and irrepressible bird is a Southern California native, and is one of the rare people who really loves L.A. Her favorite song is "I Gotta Be Me."

Contact BJ Gallagher at www.peacockproductions.com

Visit her website for additional peacock items:

- "Peacock Experience" video training package
- "Birds of Different Feathers Work Style Assessment"
- Penguin Stress Toys (ever-so-squeezable)
- "Show Your True Colors!" feather pens

AUTHOR
WARREN H. SCHMIDT

Warren Schmidt looks like a penguin and likes to think of himself as a peacock. He's really quite advanced in years ("chronologically gifted" he calls it) but has six grandchildren who force him to keep playing basketball, baseball, and tennis as if he were only middle-aged.

In his long career Warren has played many roles – from minister to psychologist, from professor to city commissioner, from researcher to screen writer. He has taught others how to do Life Planning, but his own career has been shaped by a lot of unexpected opportunities – leading him from Detroit, Michigan (where he was born), to Missouri, to New York, to Massachusetts, to Ohio, to Washington, D.C. – and finally to settle down in the San Fernando Valley in California with his family of one wife (Reggie) and four kids (now increased to a clan of sixteen). While in California he has taught at two of that state's great educational institutions, UCLA and USC. Even when he "settled down" at UCLA, however, he didn't stay with a single role, moving from the Psychology department to the Graduate School of Management, where he ended up as dean of Executive Education. After twenty-two years, however, Warren finally became a mature, dependable professor of Public administration at the University of Southern California (but not quite a penguin, he insists!).

Warren likes to write – particularly with someone else. He first tasted the fun of collaboration when he and Bob Tannenbaum wrote an article on "How to Choose a Leadership Pattern" for the *Harvard Business Review* – a management classic that has sold more than one million reprints. He has written books on teamwork with Gordon Lippitt and Paul Buchanan, monographs on managerial values with Barry Posner, and most recently, two books on Total Quality Management with Jerry Finnigan of the

Xerox Corporation: *The Race Without a Finish Line* and *TQManager*. When BJ Gallagher and Warren teamed up to write this Peacock tale, it began another delightful creative partnership leading to two more penguin books and videos.

A major dimension was added to Warren's life in 1969 when he wrote a parable about divisiveness in America titled "Is It Always Right to Be Right?" Its appearance in *The Los Angeles Times* attracted the attention of four film producers (as well as Ted Kennedy and Spiro Agnew). Steven Bosustow (of *Mr. Magoo* fame) made an animated film of the parable; Orson Wells narrated it – and it won an Academy Award in 1971. As an "instant expert" on films, Warren was invited to become an advisor for CRM Films – and has never stopped writing and advising. (CRM Films produced an animated video of Warren and BJ's *A Peacock in the Land of Penguins* in 1995, as well as a sequel, *Pigeon Holed in the Land of Penguins* in 1999.

Warren is retired and lives in Westwood, a section of Los Angeles.

If you have enjoyed this book we invite you to check out our entire collection of gift books, with free inspirational movies, at **www.simpletruths.com.**

You'll discover it's a great way to inspire *friends* and *family,* or to thank your best *customers* and *employees.*

Our products are *not available in bookstores ... only direct.* Therefore, when you purchase a gift from Simple Truths you're giving something that can't be found elsewhere!

For more information, please visit us at:
www.simpletruths.com

Or call us toll free…
800-900-3427

Show your
  true colors!